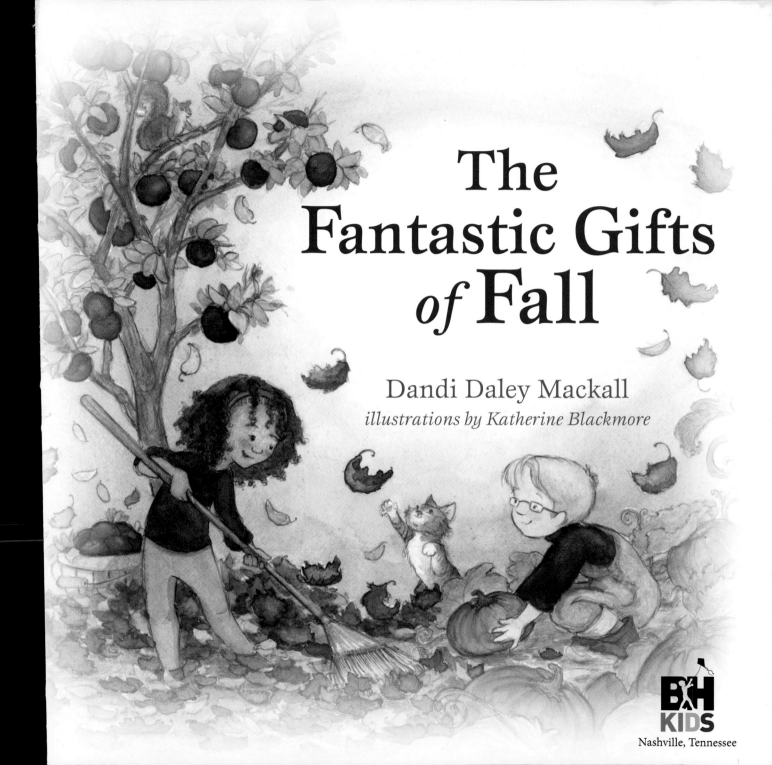

The
Fantastic Gifts
of Fall

Dandi Daley Mackall

illustrations by Katherine Blackmore

B&H KIDS

Nashville, Tennessee

Dewey Decimal Classification: J508.2
Subject Heading: AUTUMN \ SEASONS \
THANKSGIVING DAY

ISBN: 978-1-4336-8237-7
Printed in China
1 2 3 4 5 6 7 8 - 18 17 16 15 14

For Ellie Hendren, sweet in all seasons.
—Dandi

For Heather—and in joyful celebration of autumn!
—Kathy

May his land be blessed by the LORD
with the dew of heaven's bounty . . .
with the bountiful harvest from the sun
and the abundant yield of the seasons.
—DEUTERONOMY 33:13–14

God created everything—
Summer, autumn, winter, spring.
See what autumn blessings bring. . . .
Thank You, God, for autumn!

Call it "fall," as some folks say.
Autumn's here! Hip, hip, hooray!
Frisky, brisky, sometimes gray—
Thank You, God, for autumn.

The Lord makes the rain clouds, and He will give them showers of rain and crops in the field for everyone.
—ZECHARIAH 10:1

Geese fly in a crooked V,
Ducks quack-quacking merrily.
You made everything I see.
Thank You, God, for autumn.

But ask the animals, and they will instruct you;
ask the birds of the sky, and they will tell you.
—Job 12:7

Leaves change colors. Bye-bye, green!
Reds and yellows on the scene.
Pears and pumpkins! Peachy keen!
Thank You, God, for autumn.

Let the fields and everything in them exult.
Then all the trees of the forest will shout for joy.
—PSALM 96:12

Autumn tree, my favorite nook,
Curled up with my favorite book—
Peaceful everywhere I look.
Thank You, God, for autumn.

Then My people will dwell in a peaceful place, in safe and secure dwellings.
—Isaiah 32:18

Autumn harvest, smell the hay!
Hayrides the old-fashioned way;
Squirrels and rabbits come to play.
Thank You, God, for autumn.

My mouth will declare Yahweh's praise;
let every living thing praise His holy name forever and ever.
—Psalm 145:21

I taste blessings everywhere:
Apple, peach, banana, pear,
Homemade cookies, baked with care.
Thank You, God, for autumn.

Taste and see that the LORD is good.
How happy is the man who takes refuge in Him!
—PSALM 34:8

Leaves are falling. Catch a few!
Brown, instead of green like new.
Crackly, crunchy 'neath my shoe.
Thank You, God, for autumn.

For the sun rises with its scorching heat and dries up the grass;
its flower falls off, and its beautiful appearance is destroyed.
—JAMES 1:11

Horseback riding, "Giddyup!"
Toss a stick; "Go fetch it, pup."
Cats go marching—hup, hup, hup.
Thank You, God, for autumn.

You open Your hand and satisfy the desire
of every living thing.
—Psalm 145:16

Finally, it's Thanksgiving Day!
Family come from miles away.
Don't eat yet—it's time to pray.
Thank You, God, for autumn.

All You have made will thank You, LORD;
the godly will praise You.
—PSALM 145:10

Thanks for family, old and new.
Thanks for food and blessings too.
All good things come straight from You!
Thank You, God, for autumn.

He did what is good by giving you rain from heaven
and fruitful seasons and satisfying your hearts with food and happiness.
—ACTS 14:17

Squirrels store acorns. It's a sign.
You hide your nuts. I'll eat mine.
Autumn gifts are mighty fine.
Thank you, God, for autumn.

All eyes look to You, and You give them their food at the proper time.
—PSALM 145:15

"Bye-bye!" Birdies leave the nest.
Earth must take its beauty rest.
Praise the Lord from east to west!
Thank You, God, for autumn.

Therefore, in the east honor the LORD!
In the islands of the west honor the name of Yahweh, the God of Israel.
—ISAIAH 24:15

Icy breeze is pretty numbing.
Hear that wind? It sounds like drumming.
Autumn's fading. Winter's coming.
Thank You, God, for autumn.

What road leads to the place where light is dispersed?
Where is the source of the east wind that spreads across the earth?
—JOB 38:24

Remember:
Give thanks in everything.
—1 Thessalonians 5:18

Read:
Way back in Genesis 1:9–13, when God was creating the earth, He made sure that we would have much to be thankful for at harvest time. On that third day, He thought up all sorts of different plants, vegetables, and fruit trees to give us lots of yummy food to eat. He even threw in the colorful, falling leaves as a bonus! When you think of the bounty of this season, be sure to thank the God of all seasons, the God who created a beautiful autumn and a plentiful harvest just for you.

Think:
1. Why do you think God made the seasons?
2. What are your favorite things about autumn?
3. If you could make the Thanksgiving menu, what would be on it?
4. List three blessings that you can only enjoy during the fall.
5. What are you most thankful for?

Do:
Create a Tree of Thanks.
1. Collect two or three different kinds of leaves.
2. Trace the leaves onto colored paper and cut them out until you have five leaves.
3. On brown paper, draw and cut out a tree trunk with five branches.
4. Write the words of 1 Thessalonians 5:18 on the trunk.
5. Write one thing that you're thankful for on each leaf. Thank God for each one!
6. Tape or glue one leaf onto each branch.
7. Hang your Tree of Thanks where you can see it and be thankful all season long!

Look at the blessings all around.
Give thanks!